FOX ON A COLD TIN ROOF

By

Raymond Lord

Dedicated to: Kristina, Anthony, Amanda, and Adrianna

The Big Snow!

Today is going to be a good day! It was snowing last night when Anthony went to bed, and the weather man on television said that all schools were going to be closed the next day. This was good news!

Anthony had already made plans for the following day; he got out his snow pants, boots, hat and jacket and laid them out for the big snow day.

Anthony jumped out of bed and ran to the window in his room to make sure that the snow was still there, it was! There was snow everywhere! There was snow on the roof tops, the trees and it covered all the ground as far as one could see.

Suddenly Anthony saw something strange, he could not believe his eyes and had to rub them to make sure.

Yes, he was not imagining it. A fox was sleeping all curled in a ball on the roof of the neighbor's shed.

Anthony ran quickly to tell Dad what he had seen. "Dad!" said Anthony. "A fox is on top of our neighbor's shed!"

Anthony's Dad woke up and jumped out of bed. "A fox?" said Dad. "That can't be!" Dad looked confused. "Go to the window and see," Anthony told him.

Dad and Anthony went to the window to see if the fox was still there, and it was.

"Wow, a fox is on top of our neighbor's shed! Let me get the camera," said Dad. Dad told Anthony to stay by the window to keep an eye on the fox.

While Dad went for the camera Anthony kept a good watch and reported back everything that the fox was doing on the shed.

Anthony reported that the fox was looking down from the roof of the shed and that he was getting closer and closer to the edge, until it took a step and fell down into the soft snow, right into our backyard!

Anthony called out, "The fox is in our yard!" and we all came to see. Amanda and Adrianna also came to see.

There it was in our backyard the same fox, but this time it did not jump down into the drain like other days. The snow had covered most of the entrance to the drain and it looked like the fox could not find its hole.

The fox was pacing around the drain as if it was looking for something, sniffing and pacing. Things did not look good. Was the fox hurt? Maybe it could no longer find its home.

The fox even began digging frantically in the snow, but it was not anywhere near the entrance to the drain. It was very cold outside and foxes have to sleep during the day since they are out hunting at night.

The kids told Dad that he had to go outside to help the poor fox that had to get home.

They told him that he had to help the fox by shoveling the snow that was covering the entrance to the fox's home

Dad tried to convince them that the fox was ok; he said "The fox is fine, they have fur and live outdoors", but the kids insisted.

After a long while of digging in the snow, the little fox laid itself down in the snow and again curled into a ball and looked like it had fallen asleep.

This really bothered everyone because it looked like that poor fox was going to freeze out in the cold.

Mom came to see how the fox was doing and said that the fox could be in trouble because it was now laying down in the snow.

"Ok", said Dad, "I will go outside to help the fox", and the kids all cheered.

Dad got out his snow pants, boots, hat and jacket, and then began getting ready to go outside.

Dad got everything that he needed to go outside, including the snow shovel from the garage. We were all just hoping that the fox would run away and not jump on our Dad! Dad said, " I hope so too!"

Dad had a plan, he said that the fox would run away if it saw him and he could then dig out the hole while the fox was away.

He finally made it to the backdoor and opened it to go out. He was all bundled up and ready for anything.

When the fox saw our Dad, it suddenly jumped up and disappeared down into the hole in a flash.

Going…

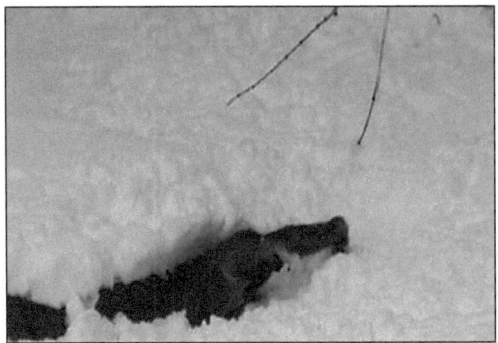

Going…

Gone!

It turns out that the fox was just enjoying its own snow day and was relaxing outside its den!

The kids all laughed because they thought it was funny that their Dad got all dressed to go outside and the fox made fun of him.

Dad thought it was pretty funny too, but explained to the children that they should always try and help animals that look like it may be in trouble by telling a grown up and that they had all done the right thing.

THE END!

Copyright © 2011

PanaTechnica Publishing

www.PanaTechnica.com

Printed in the USA

ISBN-13: 9780615461588

ISBN-10: 0615461581

Library of Congress Control Number: 2011904995

www.ingramcontent.com/pod-product-compliance
Lightning Source LLC
Chambersburg PA
CBHW041745040426
42444CB00001B/36